Christmas

Ten Poems for Dark W

ex libris

Candlestick Press

Published by:
Candlestick Press,
Diversity House, 72 Nottingham Road, Arnold, Nottingham UK NG5 6LF
www.candlestickpress.co.uk

Design and typesetting by Diversity Creative Marketing Solutions Ltd.,
www.diversity.agency

Printed by Ratcliff & Roper Print Group, Nottinghamshire, UK

Cover illustration © Sarah Young, 2018
www.sarah-young.co.uk

Candlestick Press monogram © Barbara Shaw, 2008

Donation to Starlight Children's Foundation
www.starlight.org.uk

ISBN 978 1 907598 71 5

Acknowledgements:

Thanks are due to all the copyright holders cited below for their kind permission:

Nancy Campbell, poem as yet unpublished, by kind permission of the author

Niall Campbell, poem as yet unpublished, by kind permission of the author

John Clegg, poem as yet unpublished, by kind permission of the author

Tony Curtis, poem as yet unpublished, by kind permission of the author

Katherine Gallagher, poem as yet unpublished, by kind permission of the author

Stephen Keeler, poem as yet unpublished, by kind permission of the author

Zaffar Kunial, poem as yet unpublished, by kind permission of the author

Hannah Lowe, poem as yet unpublished, by kind permission of the author

Kim Moore, poem as yet unpublished, by kind permission of the author

Amali Rodrigo, poem as yet unpublished, by kind permission of the author

Contents

Christmas Lights

They're putting up the lights strung out on poles
along the harbour wall, the dark young lads
in oily overalls; and there's a tree
built out of creels out at The Point, as though
a pagan pendant on a flimsy string
of beads, defiant, and alluring as
the Sirens' phantom lighthouse.
                              And upstairs
in dim bedrooms the girls undress and dress;
the boys smirk at the mirror mouthing chat-
up lines from movies.
                              Now the village is
en fête: dressed for a party in the dark,
across the fields, along uneven paths,
a low-roofed barn with steamed-up windows and
a fiddler and her band. And Christmas lights.

Stephen Keeler

Unity Brass Band, Leicester

When I walk past a brass band playing carols
I think of us all back then, those evenings

walking the streets to stand under a pool of light -
Coventry Carol, In the Bleak Midwinter –

the carol books with hand-drawn angels on the front,
the likes of which I've never found again,

how sometimes I stood apart in the dark,
because I knew each carol off by heart,

watched the band gathered round the light,
how our conductor could play anything

but often played soprano just for fun, the descants
floating up into the night, not written down,

straight from his heart and made of light.
One night it was so cold, all the valves froze solid,

first the bass and euphonium, then the baritones
stopped speaking. Like animals dying from thirst

they fell in order of size, tenor horns next, then cornets
one by one, and his the last to stop its song,

one last breath of silent, silent night.

Kim Moore

A Winter's Tale of the Present in a Matchbox

Did its case say *strike softly, away from the body*? If I remember right
it was ENGLAND'S GLORY. With a ship. Not long as Vestas.
But it weighed improbably. The weight of beginning, which was
everything. Present in a matchbox. Here's the story. Dad worked
nights in a factory. Joseph Lucas Ltd. Those words lay lightly, on
an unembarrassed folder I'd take in to secondary school, but this
time was before. Primary years, when the union's Christmas party,
at Lucas's, felt like a day trip to Willy Wonka's. My father made
car batteries. A mystery to me. On the way from work he'd bring
the daylight with him, and that day's *Mirror* with all its headlines
and a packet of crisps. If awake, I'd wait at the top of the stairs
in the unlit dawn to hear morning turn the key. I'm getting ahead
of myself. One Christmas, at my school, St John's C of E, before
the holidays, theirs and in a way ours, teachers set a game for all
ages, every class. To fill a small matchbox with objects, as many
as we could, and no two objects the same. And for the first time,
my father who wrote in slow capitals, helped with my homework.
His factory was streets away from my school in Sparkhill, a short
walk, but that doesn't convey the cosmic difference. One morning.
Here. Open your hand. Not crisps. I felt the weight of his factory.
Everyone on his floor had helped. Each adding their own lexicon.
Each grade of tiny screw, or washer, or cog, or bolt, packed, piled,
anonymous and proud. An assembled load, like the first singularity
before any difference explodes in metal or matter, or the grammar
school Latin my mother knew, a mass foreign to me as *prima luce*
though I'd heard of Lucifer. And Lucas's. How heavy light's cargo.
Heavy as when words box more meanings, compact in the drawer
of one sound. Story. Or. Our. Material. Kashmir. Light. Grammar.
Assembly. Gravity. Present. Pronounced. Weight. Holi. Spirit. Sun.
Mass. Let. Be. Lux. One. I *won. By a long way*, the head teacher said
before the whole assembly. Overnight, Dad's word spread like a lit
fuse in the din of the factory floor, to dawn. *By long way. We won. Won.*

Zaffar Kunial

Christmas Eve Fire at Barrington Cement Works

Customers of the Plough at Shepreth
In '86 photographed
Spilling out into the carpark and toasting
The orangey buzz in the background

A good fire cosily distant
From anyone's anything
Wasp nest in fusebox
Cement sacks tender as crêpe-paper

(This is our guesswork)
The barman passes down the photo
He knew the nightwatchman
Who trudged a long mile over the field

After the phones had failed
His back to the fire
Cupping his own smoke
And mulling the meaning of *tidings*

John Clegg

Museum of Angels

The angels arrive earlier each year.

These days the sycamore holds both
summer and autumn; a low brocade

of gold, and at the pinnacle young
green reaching for an evermore.

How we too must live like this, holding
on and letting go, while the men are spidering

up brick walls to set angels above us
and for weeks we are children

eyes trained on a constellation, beginning
to know our own particular angel,

her garnet heart, her peacock-blue fur,
her tiny eyes like the distant blinks of icicles,

and all the while a star climbs the dark
stair to catch a finer glimpse of us,

centuries passing as the three wise men wander,
searching for lost children.

Amali Rodrigo

Sugar Nanna

...they saw that the little house was built entirely from bread
with a roof made of cake, and the windows were made of clear sugar –
Hansel and Gretel

Even the thought of you fills my mouth with sugar.
Brittle snap on teeth – your gingerbread
in baubled paper, or wet on the tongue –

the thick black jam we slathered under marzipan.
In all your bowls, I licked, sat in the pantry,
or in the parlour, sucking Simpkins travel sweets,

lights like sugar almonds on the Christmas tree.
And your sweetness was perennial –
school day mornings, the war-time treacle

of your voice would lure me down to honeycomb
from Romford Market. I knew nothing of the battle –
Mum hating you, you hating my father, his colour,

rotting my milk molars, on purpose?
But I was indiscriminate, desirous –
on Christmas Eve, when dad bought spears

of sugarcane from Seven Sisters and held them
to his lips to taste Jamaica, I wanted one –
snow lolly, light sabre. I didn't hear

your summons – syrup-steam, rising up.
I'd take my sugar from any spoon or duct.
I stayed upstairs and sucked.

Hannah Lowe

Hush

The truth is, the bushes were
laden with bright red berries,
the heavens lit with stars,

and though it was deep winter,
green leaves unfurled
like small hands opening.

Trees stood still. Above them,
the curve of two bare hills softened.
Rivers in torrent quietened,

appeared to hold their breath.
Even the donkey in the corner
of the stable knelt, lay down.

Whereas the night before,
our hands were cold
and water in the well had frozen,

that night the air was honied,
as if a veil of wild heather
had fallen over the town.

Somebody said it was
miraculous.
But is that the word for it?

The world so hushed
you could hear
a new born baby cry.

Tony Curtis

Northern lights

Sometimes you can sense them,
Guðny says. In winter she wakes
at midnight to an intense silence
as if the town is stalking itself,
and she knows the skies will be bright
as butter. She opens the window
to feel the cold air rising from the snow
and sits on the low sill, half-
dreaming, watching the lights churn
over the hills, whisky gold in her glass.

When he's not working nights
Björn likes to borrow Guðny's car
and drive out of town. He believes
you can always see the lights better
in the next valley, but you have to hurry
before they disappear. On the cliff road
he'll switch the headlights off while his eyes
adjust to the dark. Down by the fjord
he stops, lies back on the warm bonnet,
listening to the heat shields tick.

When her husband's away at sea
Alice often walks to the beach
with her camera set to manual
and a spare battery. If the tide's out
she fixes a tripod among the small black rocks
which smell of kelp. Each time the shutter clicks
it captures new magnetic patterns.
Back home she patiently scrolls
through hundreds of thumbnails,
deletes them one by one, keeping the best.

Far out on the North Banks
the floodlit deck of Sindri's trawler
is rich with fish. He heads for home:
the lights of his town are hidden
so it's good to see the aurora
soaring over those mountains,
and the slow sweep of the beam
from Siglunes lighthouse in the east.
A tiny satellite blinks above him
collecting data for the storm report.

Birna is tired, there's so much to do
before the family visits. As she hangs
glittering stars upon her tree
the weather forecast promises
perfect cloud cover, but tonight
she's got no desire to look outside:
the aurora will continue circling
the world, and someone else will watch
its fires dance, while she remembers
the nights long gone.

Nancy Campbell

Skater on the Lake

I sometimes think about a lake
gone frozen over, reeds to bank,
sliding rocks out to test its bearing,
the skater checks how the fresh ice

will hold the skater – the slight cracking
beneath the tried, failed pirouette;
pledging to movement, when the heart's
long since been complicated by

its own sure reeling, love to love
to love – stillness leaves the ice unscored,
perfect, the skater sews one hundred
bright flaws into the lake's faint light.

Niall Campbell

Les Lumières de Paris

From way off out of darkness, we saw it:
the city's glittering heart, its promised streets garlanded,
radiating out in the frosty air: Place de la Concorde,
Madeleine, Notre Dame, Tour Eiffel, Quartier Latin,
Abbesses and the climb up to Montmartre where
Van Gogh had toiled under these lights,
breath of the Seine edging the city's heartbeat,
the famous bridges encapsulating journeys, haloed;

tourists clasping history, with Sacré Coeur, this great basilica
built following the Franco-Prussian war, overlooking all.
The flower-stall holders calling for customers, along with
the crowded cafés, restaurants, bars, pâtisseries, open
to sell their wares, everything illumined as though evening light
rivalled daytime, and a meal out to celebrate *the fêtes*
were an invitation to savour food for soul and eye – almost
as if the whole city were dining out in one awaited spectacle,

sharing expectation and moments with locals and visitors:
lovers, parents and children: scarved, mittened,
the sense of the party carrying on, and Père Noel
still sky-jingling, turning the day on its head –
everything framed by bonhomie and Christmas markets,
chance meetings, so many drawn to the celebrations,
this gaiety of blending – music, welcoming, reclaiming colours
under the lights, as though nothing could go unnoticed

in this walk-walk city. We had seen the world hush
for the shortest day, the skies darkening over.
And now the solstice gloom had turned to light,
holding us, real as our venturing, retrieving meanings
shaped by days drawing in, beckoning us towards
blazes of colour, neon: illuminations
that would stay with us for the year to come.

Katherine Gallagher